UNITED ARAB EMIRATES

MAJOR WORLD NATIONS

UNITED ARAB EMIRATES

Julia Johnson

CHELSEA HOUSE PUBLISHERS
Philadelphia

Chelsea House Publishers

First Printing.

1 3 5 7 9 8 6 4 2

Library of Congress Cataloging-in-Publication Data

Johnson, Julia
[U.A.E]
United Arab Emirates / Julia Johnson.
p. cm. — (Major world nations)
Includes index.
Summary: An overview of the history, geography, economy, government,
people, and culture of United Arab Emirates.
ISBN 0-7910-5402-0 (hc)
1. United Arab Emirates—Juvenile literature. [1. United Arab
Emirates.] I. Title. II. Series.
DS247.T8J64   1999
953.57—dc21   99-11868
CIP

ACKNOWLEDGEMENTS

The Author and Publishers are grateful to the following organizations and individuals
for permission to reproduce copyright illustrations in this book:
Embassy of the United Emirates, London; Hutchison Photo Library; Ministry of
Information of the United Arab Emirates; Norman D. Price/Vidocq Photo Library;
Helene Rogers; Frank Spooner Pictures.

CONTENTS

PERSIAN GULF

QATAR

DAS ISLAND

Jebel Dhanna
Ruwais

ABU

LIWA OAS

IRAQ

KUWAIT

IRAN

PERSIAN GULF

QATAR

OMAN

SAUDI
ARABIA

SAUDI ARABIA

FACTS AT A GLANCE

Land and People

Official Name	United Arab Emirates
Location	Middle East, bordering the Gulf of Oman and the Persian (Arabian) Gulf
Area	30,000 square miles (77,000 square kilometers)
Climate	Desert, cooler in the mountains
Capital	Abu Dhabi
Other Cities	Dubai, Fujairah, Khor Fakkan
Population	2,303,088
Mountains	Hajar
Highest Point	Jabal Yibir (1,527 meters)
Official Language	Arabic
Other Languages	Farsi (Persian), English, Hindu, Urdu
Religions	Muslim, 96 percent; Christian or Hindu, 4 percent
Literacy Rate	79.2 percent

Average Life Expectancy	74.93 years

Economy

Natural Resources	Petroleum, natural gas
Division of Labor Force	Services, 65 percent; industry and commerce, 30 percent; agriculture, 5 percent
Agricultural Products	Dates, watermelon, poultry, dairy products, vegetables
Industries	Petroleum, fishing, petrochemicals, pearling, handicrafts
Major Imports	Manufactured goods, machinery and transportation equipment, chemicals, food
Major Exports	Crude oil, natural gas, dried fish, dates
Major Trading Partners	Japan, South Korea, Singapore, India, Iran, United States, Italy, United Kingdom
Currency	Emirian dirham

Government

Form of Government	Federation
Government Bodies	Supreme Council, made up of the seven emirs of the seven emirates; Federation National Council, made up of 40 members appointed by the emirs
Formal Head of State	President
Head of Government	Prime minister

HISTORY AT A GLANCE

3000 B.C. A farming community inhabits the lands on the Persian Gulf. The land is wetter with more rainfall than present-day and allows for the growing of more crops.

900-500 B.C. An Iron Age town exists in the Dubai region. A major trade route crosses the Persian Gulf area. Irrigation channels called *falaj* are dug to allow for farming on the oases.

7th century A.D. The Islam religion spreads throughout the area.

early 16th century Portuguese traders take control of the Persian Gulf and takeover trade in the area. Their presence is bitterly resisted by the many tribes.

17th-18th centuries Piracy is common in the Persian Gulf region. The strongest tribes are the Qawasim and the Bani Yas. The Qawasim are called pirates by the British because they raid the British ships fighting against British control in the area.

1820 The British destroy the main fleet of the Qawasim. A treaty is signed and the British establish an army station at Ras al Khaimah.

10

1853	The British sign another treaty with the rulers of the coastal tribes promising to protect the area from outside attack. The coastal area is now called Trucial Coast.
1892	The sheikhs (chiefs) of the tribes sign another agreement with the British not to deal with any other foreign power. This "exclusive agreement" strengthens Britain's hold on the area.
1951	The British form a military force called the Trucial Oman Scouts whose purpose is to keep order in the area and to assist with exploration for oil. A council is formed made up of the sheikhs of the area.
1958	Oil is discovered in Abu Dhabi.
1960s	The Emirates rapidly become one of the richest nations in the world due to the oil.
1968	Britain agrees to withdraw from the Persian Gulf area in 1971.
1968-1971	Meetings are held between the individual tribes or emirates that live in the Gulf area to negotiate joining into a single federation. Abu Dhabi, Dubai, Sharjah, Ajman, Umm al Qawain, and Fujeirah choose to join. Ras al Khaimah, Bahrain and Qatar choose to remain independent. (Ras al Khaimah will join in 1972.)
1971	On December 2 the United Arab Emirates (UAE) becomes an independent country.
1971-1990s	The UAE is a stable and peaceful country that becomes a world business center.
1990-1991	The UAE sides with the anti-Iraq coalition in the Gulf War, strengthening its ties with the west.

11

1

A Land of Contrasts and Surprises

The United Arab Emirates—the name might conjure up the traditional image of Arabs riding through the sands on their camels. Since the discovery of petroleum, which has put the country on the map, most people would also include a backdrop of oil rigs. There certainly is sand—lots of it—and camels—many of them—and oil—plenty of it. But there is much more besides. The UAE is a land of contrasts and surprises, of old and new living in harmony side by side, and most of all it is a land of welcome.

The United Arab Emirates, a federation of seven emirates, came into being in December 1971. Before independence, the area was under British control through a series of treaty arrangements dating back to 1820. From one of them, the General Treaty on Maritime Truce, the area received the name "The Trucial States."

Lying on the southeast corner of the Arabian peninsula, the UAE enjoys the longest coast on the Persian Gulf, extending

Traditional *dhows* (cargo ships) and modern buildings side by side in Dubai.

approximately 370 miles (600 kilometers) in the north and over 60 miles (100 kilometers) on the Arabian Sea in the east. Excluding the islands, it covers an area of about 30,000 square miles (77,000 square kilometers). From east to west the emirates are Abu Dhabi, Dubai, Sharjah, Ajman, Umm al Qawain, Ras al Khaimah, and Fujeirah. Six of them lie on the coast of the Persian Gulf while the seventh, Fujeirah, is situated on the eastern coast of the peninsula and has direct access to the Gulf of Oman in the Indian

13

Boats moored in the harbor at Knor Fakkan. The mountains in the background are in neighboring Oman.

Ocean. This is an area of very shallow seas, offshore islands, and coral reefs. The UAE is geologically a stable zone and there is little likelihood of major earthquakes or volcanic eruptions.

Qatar lies to the west of the UAE, and Oman to the east. The UAE also has a large boundary with Saudi Arabia on the northern fringes of the Rub al Khali, or Empty Quarter. Abu Dhabi is the largest emirate, with an area of over 25,000 square miles (65,000 square kilometers). Abu Dhabi town is also the capital of the UAE. It lies on a triangular island, linked to the mainland by two bridges. The emir (ruler) of Abu Dhabi is the country's president. The most important port is Dubai because of its position on one of the rare deep creeks of the area. The emir of Dubai is the country's vice-president and, since April 1979, he has also been the prime minister. These two emirs together with the rulers of the other five emirates, make up the Supreme Council of Rulers of the federal government.

The UAE is classed as a desert because it receives less than 10 inches (25 centimeters) of rain a year. One-eighth of the world is desert, and the largest, hottest deserts are in the Arab world.

Some plant life has adapted to desert conditions. Seeds, protected by tough coverings, can be blown around for years waiting for moisture or a suitable spot to germinate. Some plants have few leaves so that little water is lost to the air. Some have developed spines to stop animals from eating them. Others, known as succulents, have fleshy stems in which water is stored. Still others grow very long roots to penetrate the soil down to the water table. The roots of the mesquite, for example, can grow over 115 feet (35 meters) long and those of the tamarisk over 164 feet (50 meters).

Soils in the UAE are generally coarse and sandy and contain little organic matter. *Sabkah* is the name for the salty mudflats which run the length of the coastline. With the exception of the oases, most of the emirates are so arid that sustained agriculture is not possible without artificial irrigation. Some protection against high winds and high summer temperatures is also necessary. An oasis is a fertile spot where water is more abundant and settled agriculture is possible. The largest oases are to be found in the emirate of Abu Dhabi. Al Ain is the most fertile and extensive oasis, while the Liwa is a string of small oases on the edge of the Rub al Khali. The Liwa was a regular and vital stopping point for caravans crossing the desert. Lush greenery is also to be found at Al Dhaid

The emirs (sheikhs) of the area rule each of the seven emirates.

oasis in the emirate of Sharjah, at Hatta in Dubai, and at the agricultural center of Umm al Qawain at Falaj al Mualla oasis. Ras al Khaimah, the most northerly of the emirates, is the most fertile of them all.

Most of the UAE is flat, but to the east the barren, rugged Hajar mountains divide the country into the Dhahira, or Gulf coast, and the Batinah coast on the Indian Ocean. The mountains are full of steep-sided valleys known as *wadis*. When rain falls, it can come in a sudden localized downpour and can cause flash floods. Sudden torrents carry away soil from the dried-up *wadis* and make them even deeper. There are no permanent rivers in the Gulf area and only a few short streams in the mountains.

Much of the land is covered with sand. Often sand is blown into dunes. Sand dunes are a dominant feature of the landscape. Crescent-shaped sand dunes, called *barchans* (pronounced "barkaans"), are formed by the wind blowing in one direction. Strong winds and sandstorms are common. June usually sees the onset of seasonal northwesterly winds over most of the Gulf area, known generally as the "forty-day shamal." At this time of the year, the climate seems choking and oppressive. Localized eddies swirl dust, leaves, and paper about. In the central Gulf area, the summer *shamal* blows with varying strength. It can occasionally reach gale force with rough seas. Sometimes a thick dust haze blows from the dust bowl in Iraq.

From October to mid-May, the weather is ideal with clear, warm sunny days and pleasantly cool nights. Fog can occur at night, especially on the coast. From May onward the temperature rises steadily. The average temperature in July and August is around 105 degrees Fahrenheit (40 degrees Celsius), but it can reach as high as 118 degrees Fahrenheit (48 degrees Celsius). This, combined with a high level of humidity, makes for a very uncomfortable summer. From June to August, humidity levels average 97 percent. In such conditions, strenuous outdoor activity can be dangerous. However, houses, shops, offices, and even cars, are

17

Desert flowers. Despite the arid and harsh environment of much of the UAE, some plants and animals are able to survive.

almost always fully air-conditioned. The summer climate is too hot even for people who like sunbathing.

One world record which the Persian Gulf can claim is that of the highest sea surface temperatures. In the central and eastern Gulf, summer sea temperatures reach 93-95 degrees Fahrenheit (34-35 degrees Celsius). The highest temperature recorded to date is 96.8 degrees Fahrenheit (36 degrees Celsius). In lagoons, the temperature can exceed 104 degrees Fahrenheit (40 degrees Celsius) which makes swimming extremely uncomfortable. A dip in the sea ceases to be refreshing when the sea temperature is higher than skin temperature.

It is estimated that the total UAE population is about two million but only 25 percent are actually citizens, or nationals as they are called. The official language is Arabic, although English is widely spoken. All the native inhabitants are Muslim, mainly of the Sunni sect. (The Sunni are one of two sects to emerge after the death of the Prophet Muhammad due to a difference of opinion over who should be Muhammad's successor. The other sect are called Shi'ite Muslims.) With their background of navigation and exploration, the ancestors of the Arabs of the Emirates can be traced back to many parts of the world, from Aden to Zanzibar. Skin color in the Emirates varies from light brown to black, and facial characteristics are equally varied. This cosmopolitan heritage leads to a cosmopolitan outlook.

There are also many non-Arab immigrant workers. In the coastal towns there are many Iranians, Indians, Pakistanis, Baluchis, and blacks. The latter are descended from slaves who were transported from Africa during the course of several cen-

Barchans—crescent-shaped sand dunes formed by the wind blowing consistently in one direction.

turies of slave trading. Other expatriates, including Westerners, make up about 5.5 percent of the total population.

The UAE has developed at an amazing pace. Progress in education and health facilities, for example, has been dramatic. The country was fortunate to be blessed with large quantities of oil, and revenue from oil dominates the economy. Since oil was discovered the UAE's revenue from petroleum has grown significantly, and the economy expanded very rapidly.

The UAE belongs to both the 13-member Organization of Petroleum Exporting Countries (OPEC) and the nine-member Organization of Arab Petroleum Exporting Countries (OAPEC). During the 1980s, oil production fell off as a result of a deliberate policy of consolidating resources, and because of OPEC production cutbacks. But now the UAE is currently producing 2.5 million barrels a day.

It is due to the far-sightedness of its rulers that the UAE has achieved so much in so short a time, but underlying this progress is the firm foundation of Islam.

2

Digging into the Past

Archaeological findings show that there was an advanced civilization in the coastal area of what is now the UAE as long ago as the third millennium B.C. The community traded with the inhabitants of the Indus Valley in Pakistan to the east, and of Mesopotamia to the west. The Gulf has always been a waterway for trade. Assyrian and Babylonian merchants once passed this way, with cargoes of frankincense, spices, pearls, metals, and timbers. A Mesopotamian clay tablet speaks of "fishes' eyes," which are the pearls for which the Gulf was famed for the next 3,000 years. The lives of the Gulf peoples have always centered around the sea. Their *dhows*, great seafaring ships, have changed little in construction over the centuries. The craft of *dhow*-building continues today on the beaches of Ajman.

In ancient times the region had a very different climate. There was more rain, which meant that it was easier to grow crops. This encouraged communities to settle. Major excavations at Hili, near Al Ain, have unearthed seeds and stalks of wheat, barley, oats, and sorghum, as well as date stones and melon seeds. These show that a settled pastoral community inhabited the area in about 3000 B.C. The presence of fossils in the dunes also indicates that the shoreline was once considerably further inland.

Tombs have also been unearthed, along with a copper smelting site, a well, and irrigation or drainage channels. One large, bee-hive-shaped stone structure, with relief carvings, has been restored, and can be seen today in the Hili Gardens public park. Pottery and soapstone vessels were found in the tombs, along with cornelian (a reddish-yellow semiprecious stone) and shell beads, and copper and bronze arrowheads.

Another major settlement and tomb site, dating from approximately 2700 B.C., is at Umm al Nar, near Abu Dhabi. This was unearthed in the mid-1950s, and was the first archaeological site

Dhows, the traditional ships of the Gulf, have changed little in design and are still built on the beaches of the emirate of Ajman as they have been for many centuries.

A tomb at Hili, near Al Ain, dating from about 3000 B.C.

to be discovered in the area. Engravings on a tomb here include pictures of camels. Camels and donkeys were probably familiar animals at this time. It is generally accepted that the camel became domesticated during the third millennium B.C. Artifacts found at these sites suggest that the population engaged in fishing, weaving, and wheat growing. They also show that the inhabitants had connections with other sites across the Gulf—for example, Tepe Yahya in Iran and the Indus Valley in Pakistan. Main exports from the UAE were soapstone vessels and copper. Evidence suggests that the peninsula of northern Oman and the UAE was the

23

copper-producing country known as Magan, which is mentioned in old Mesopotamian inscriptions.

Excavations in Ras al Khaimah emirate have revealed that the ancient palace of the legendary Queen of Sheba was probably in the village of Shimal. Many tombs dating from the second millennium B.C. stretch along the foot of the hills in this area. Evidence of trade with other regions persists—in the tombs were a broken jar from Harappa in the Indus Valley (Pakistan) and a cube-shaped weight from the same area.

Between 900 and 500 B.C., the Qusais area of Dubai was the center of an Iron Age town. In 1979, the first complete Iron Age skeleton to be found in the Lower Gulf area was unearthed. Pots buried along with the body suggest that the people of the time believed in life after death. During the Iron Age, a network of land trade routes crossed the country, and agriculture developed in oasis settlements with the spread of a system of irrigation channels known as *falaj*.

In the seventh century A.D., Islam swept through the Arabian peninsula. A trading post of the early Islamic era has been discovered in Jumeirah, which is now a fashionable residential area of Dubai. The trading post seems to have been at its height during the fifth or sixth century A.D. The settlement includes houses, a governor's residence, a marketplace, and a hunting lodge with snares for trapping wild animals, probably foxes.

Many ancient fortifications can still be found all over the Emirates. Watchtowers guarding mountain passes suggest a history of raiding.

The first complete Iron Age skeleton to be unearthed in the lower Gulf area.

Investigation into archaeological sites is encouraged both by the UAE government and by individual emirates. There is a Council of Cultural Heritage, as well as a Center for Documentation and Research. Large-scale restoration is being carried out on old buildings. For example, the historical Old Fort Palace in Abu Dhabi, built about 200 years ago, and the house of Sheikh Rashid's father, in Dubai, are being preserved.

Key discoveries from archaeological sites are displayed in the country's two museums, in Al Ain and Dubai. Another museum was built in Ras al Khaimah. Dubai Museum is housed in the Al Fihaidi fort, which is itself an historic building. It is considered to

The Old Fort Palace in Abu Dhabi, built about 200 years ago and now restored to its former glory.

be the oldest building in the emirate of Dubai and was built in about 1800. The walls were constructed of coral and shell rubble collected from the sea, cemented together with lime. Before being opened as a museum, it was part of Dubai's defenses against the attacks of neighboring tribes. Later, it became the ruler's residence and the seat of government, as well as a jail and an ammunition store.

3

From Foreign Rule to Independence

In the 15th century, the Portuguese seized control of shipping on both sides of the Indian Ocean. By the early 16th century, they had gained control of the Gulf. They took over trade from Arab and Indian merchants, shipping goods from the Far East. A garrison and customs house were set up at Julfar, now Ras al Khaimah. In 1517, the Portuguese writer Durate Barbosa wrote a description of Julfar: "There dwell persons of worth, great navigators, and wholesale dealers. Here is a very great fishery as well of seed pearls as of large pearls, and the Moors of Hormuz come hither to buy them and carry them to India and many other lands."

The Portuguese were the only Europeans in the Gulf area for many centuries. They were the scourge of Gulf seafarers, as they were cruel, and subjected their prisoners to torture and degradation. Their occupation was bitterly resisted by the two main tribal forces, the Bani Yas and the Al Qawasim.

By the end of the 16th century, Holland and Britain were also trying to establish trade in the Gulf. Portuguese supremacy gradually declined and, in 1650, the Portuguese were compelled to withdraw. There followed a period of rivalry between the Dutch and the British. Initially, the Dutch were dominant. British fortunes improved with the establishment of the British East India Company and, in 1766, the Dutch lost power.

Piracy was common in the Gulf during the 17th and 18th centuries, and reached its height at the beginning of the 19th century. From the mid-18th century onward, the strongest tribe in the Gulf area was the Qawasim of Ras al Khaimah. They ruled their territorial waters and demanded a toll from ships passing through. They earned a reputation as pirates, and the coastline became known as the "Pirate Coast." "Pirates," however, was the name given to them by the British. It is often felt today that this was an unfair description of the Qawasim in their struggles against the British East India Company.

Attacks on British ships led to British expeditions against the pirates. In 1805, the British government in India sent a force to the Gulf. As a result the first treaty between the coastal tribes and the British was signed. However, this did not suppress the Qawasim. Further expeditions followed in 1809, 1811, and 1818. In 1820, the British destroyed the main Qawasim fleet at Ras al Khaimah. They then signed a general treaty of peace with the Qawasim and all the sheikhs of the coast. A strong British squadron was stationed at Ras al Khaimah. In addition, a local political agent based at Sharjah was appointed to represent the British and to see that the sheikhs held to the signed treaty.

While the Qawasim controlled the coastal areas, the Bani Yas were the most powerful tribe in the interior. Late in the 18th century, numbers of them settled in the coastal areas of Abu Dhabi and Dubai. In 1835, they signed a truce to refrain from tribal quarrels during the all-important summer pearling season.

In 1853, the British signed a perpetual maritime treaty with the rulers of the coastal tribes and undertook to protect the states from outside attack. The coast became known as the Trucial Coast, or Trucial Oman.

Ties with Britain were further strengthened in 1892 when the sheikhs signed an "exclusive agreement," preventing them from dealing with the government of any foreign power other than Britain. This meant, for instance, that in 1911 the political agent was entitled to ask the rulers not to grant concessions to a Greek merchant who wanted to fish for pearls and sponges in the Gulf. Again, in the 1920s and 1930s the rulers were asked not to allow any foreigners to enjoy concessions for banking or oil without British approval.

In 1951, the British established a military force, known as the Trucial Oman Scouts, to keep order and to help with oil exploration in the interior. Also in 1951, a Trucial Council was established. The seven rulers met at least twice a year under the chairmanship of the British political agent in Dubai.

Oil was discovered in commercial quantities in 1958 in Abu Dhabi Emirate. The first shipment followed in 1962. With the granting of concessions to drill for oil, it became essential to define the borders between the states. As the UAE became one of the richest nations on earth, rapid development followed. Britain had previously played a peacekeeping role; now it became active in encouraging development.

In 1968, Britain announced its intention to withdraw from the Gulf area in 1971. In the same year, Sheikh Zayid of Abu Dhabi and Sheikh Rashid of Dubai met at Al Smaih on the border between their two emirates. They agreed to unite the two emirates in a single federation, which the neighboring states were also invited to join. Meetings were held with the rulers of all the present UAE states, and with those of Bahrain and Qatar, who subsequently chose to remain independent.

A parade celebrating UAE National Day. The UAE became an independent state in 1971 following Britain's withdrawal from the area.

On December 2, 1971, the United Arab Emirates became a sovereign, independent, federal state. Initially, there were six member states as Ras al Khaimah did not join the federation until February 1972. All previous treaties with Britain were replaced with a Treaty of Friendship. Membership of the Arab League and the United Nations followed. Some years later, the Gulf States Cooperation Council was established.

4

Toward an Understanding of the UAE

The people of the UAE are Muslims—followers of Islam. The word *Islam* means "submission." The religion of Islam is the main foundation of the customs and traditions of the Gulf region. To understand the people of the UAE or, for that matter, the people of the Islamic world in general, one has to first have some understanding of their religion.

Islam cannot be separated from everyday life. It is a total way of life. A Muslim believes that if he lives in accordance with the teachings of the holy Koran he will attain after-life in paradise. The Koran is the Muslim holy book, and it provides a complete guide for life. Nothing is left out. There is guidance on marriage, divorce, bringing up children, inheritance, justice, and even business conduct.

The Koran is God's word revealed to the Prophet Muhammad by the Angel Gabriel. Muhammad was born in 570 A.D. in Mecca in Saudi Arabia. He was over 40 when he started receiving messages from God. At first he was doubtful and afraid, but eventually he began to preach. Paganism and corruption were widespread at this time. In 622 A.D., the authorities forced Muhammad and his followers to leave Mecca. They decided to go to Medina. This is known as the *hejira* which means "flight" or "departure" in Arabic. (To Muslims this took place on the first day of year 1. They calculate all dates from this day, just as Christians calculate dates from the birth of Jesus.) The people of Medina immediately followed Muhammad. There were many battles between the people of Mecca and the people of Medina. Eventually, Muhammad and his followers were victorious at Badr in 630 A.D.

The Islamic religion spread quickly. It reached the UAE during the Prophet's lifetime in the middle of the seventh century. The last great battle of Islam, which established the Muslim religion in Arabia forever, was fought in 630 A.D., near Dibba in the UAE. By 732 A.D., Muslim armies had conquered the whole of the Middle East and North Africa.

A Muslim believes in one God who is called Allah. Allah is the same God who is worshiped by Jews and Christians. Muslims also believe in Jesus, but they believe that Jesus was the last of the prophets before Muhammad. Belief in Allah is one of the Five Pillars of Islam, and a Muslim affirms this belief with the statement: "There is no God but Allah, and Muhammad is his Prophet." The other four pillars are prayer, fasting, pilgrimage, and giving alms to the poor.

Five times a day, at dawn, noon, afternoon, dusk, and after

Muslims at prayer facing the holy city of Mecca.

dark, a Muslim must stop whatever he is doing to pray. He prays facing toward the holy city of Mecca, kneeling and touching the ground with his forehead in submission to Allah.

Whenever possible, he must try to go to the mosque to pray. The mosque is the Muslim place of worship. Only men go into the mosques; the women usually pray at home. Some mosques are very simple, while others are extremely elaborate. Every mosque has a tower called a minaret. In the past, a man known as a *muezzin* would call the faithful to prayer from the top of the minaret. Nowadays, loudspeakers relay his call.

There are more than 1,500 mosques throughout the UAE—an indication of a living and vibrant faith. Outside each mosque there is a fountain or running water, so that people may wash

34

before praying. Before entering the mosque, a Muslim must also take off his shoes.

The holy day of the Muslim week is Friday. The weekend starts on Thursday afternoon, and people go back to work on Saturday. On Fridays, the Imam, or spiritual leader, reads from the Koran and preaches a sermon.

Ramadan is the ninth month of the Muslim year. Islam follows a lunar calendar, and so the month of Ramadan falls at a different time each year. Ramadan commemorates the month during which

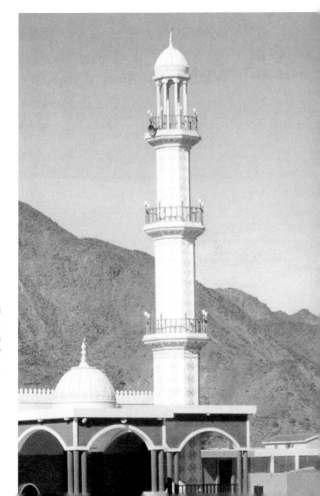

The slender minaret of a mosque in Sharjah. Nowadays the *muezzin*'s call is relayed by loudspeaker.

the Koran was first revealed to the Prophet Muhammad. It starts with the first sighting of the moon. It is traditional for groups of children to call on neighbors after dark, and be treated to Ramadan nuts and sweets. They carry lanterns called *fanoos*.

During Ramadan, a Muslim is required to fast from dawn to dusk. This does not include children. Anyone who is ill or on a journey is not expected to fast, but should make up the missed time later. It is thought that the self-denial and discipline involved in fasting nourish the soul. Fasting can be particularly difficult when Ramadan falls during the very hot summer months. In Ramadan non-Muslims are expected to respect Islamic rites and should not eat, drink, or smoke in public during daylight hours.

In the UAE, and in many other Muslim countries, the beginning and end of the daily fast is announced by the firing of a cannon. *Imsak* is the name of the meal before dawn, and *iftar* the meal after dusk. In some places a *musahir* also wanders the streets to wake people up for the *imsak* meal. He sings songs and beats his drum.

In the evening, after the daylong fasting and prayer, the streets come to life. Fruit merchants and sherbet vendors sell their wares, and many food stalls are set up on street corners. Traditionally, the fast is broken by a simple meal of dates and curd. There follows a substantial meal, which the women have probably spent much of the day preparing.

Ramadan ends at the sighting of the new moon. It is celebrated by the feast of Eid al Fitr. At dawn the men and boys gather in the

Firing a cannon to announce the end of the daily fast during Ramadan.

mosques to pray. Then they visit the sheikh to offer greetings. *Eid Mubarak* ("May your Eid be blessed") is the customary greeting.

The *musahir* usually visits the people he has helped to wake up for the *imsak* meal. They give him Eid sweets and money to thank him for his efforts during Ramadan. The children are also given presents. The women pay their respects to the sheikha, the wife of the sheikh. They visit one another and eat sweets and drink coffee. It is customary to wash in rosewater, and to inhale fragrant incense.

Every Muslim who can possibly manage it must make the pilgrimage to Mecca at least once in his lifetime. This is called the *hajj* and the pilgrim is called the *hajji*. The pilgrimage to Mecca dates back to ancient times. Muhammad included it in the religion of Islam to encourage peace between Mecca and Medina. The pilgrim enters the courtyard of the Great Mosque at Mecca wearing a white, seamless garment. He walks seven times around the Kaa'ba, a large rectangular building containing a sacred black stone, which the pilgrim kisses. The Koran says that the Kaa'ba was built by Ibrahim (Abraham) and his son Ismail to house the stone, which was given to them by the Angel Gabriel. Some say that the stone is a meteorite. The end of the *hajj* is celebrated by the Eid al Adha, or Feast of Sacrifice.

The fifth Pillar of Islam, giving alms to the poor, is called *zakat*. Each Muslim surrenders 2.5 percent of his wealth and property in order to help those less fortunate than himself. There is no begging in the UAE, since an extensive state financial aid system supports any national who cannot support himself.

The written language of the Koran is a unifying link between Muslims throughout the world. Although spoken Arabic has changed over the centuries and varies from country to country, the written word has not. Arabs today still write the same Arabic as they wrote over 1,000 years ago. The same cannot be said of the English language—the language of Chaucer, and even of Shakespeare, is difficult for us to understand today. But Arabic is very much a living language. It is written from right to left and the script is very beautiful. In fact, it is often used as an art form, since the Koran says that it is wrong to make pictures or statues of living things.

The Koran is also the major source of Islamic law, which is known as Sharia. Islamic law is also based on the hadiths, or sayings, of the Prophet Muhammad. In Sharia law, the plaintiff and defendant sit side by side before the court. Evidence on oath is acceptable since a Muslim believes that he will be eternally damned on a false oath. He would far rather take punishment under the law than risk the fires of hell. The crime rate in the UAE is low.

Islamic law allows a man to have up to four wives at the same time. The Prophet Muhammad allowed polygamy because of the number of men killed in battle in his day. Polygamy was one way of protecting widows and orphans. However, the Koran requires that all wives should be treated equally. Nowadays, polygamy is becoming less common.

5

Lifestyles and Traditions

Great importance is attached to hospitality in the UAE, as it is in all countries of the Middle East. It is considered an honor both to invite and to be invited into a home for a meal. When preparing food it is common to allow for an unexpected guest. There is an Arabic saying which goes: "If there is not more than enough, there is not enough." In the past, if a Bedouin came across a stranger in the desert it would be a matter of honor to take him home for a feast. The ultimate in traditional hospitality is to slaughter a sheep or goat for the guest. An animal killed for food must have its throat cut "in the name of Allah, Allah is most great." A woman may not slaughter, though she may guide the hand of her son if no man is available.

Cooking ability is rated highly among feminine accomplishments. A meal often begins with a variety of savory appetizers known as *mezze*. *Humus* is a puree of chickpeas mixed with olive oil, lemon, garlic, and tahini (a paste made from sesame seeds). Garlic is thought to have healing properties and to ward off the evil eye. *Tabbouleh* is a dish made from cracked wheat, parsley, tomato, mint, lemon, and spring onions. These dishes are usually eaten with scoops of flat Arab bread. *Kibbe* are meatballs. Pork is forbidden by Islam, although lamb is popular.

Locally-caught fish is still the staple diet for many Arabs in the Gulf area. The warm shallow waters offer ideal conditions for many fish. As well as commercial fishing boats, traditional crafts made of date-palm leaves can still be seen. The fishermen lower their nets around the fish and everyone wades in to drag the nets ashore. Fish is best bought from the markets early in the morning. The choice is enormous—red snapper and kingfish, lobster and huge prawns to name but a few. The fish are sold whole; outside the market, men and boys wait to gut them.

Fishermen dragging a net ashore.

The Bedouin cook meat in a hole in the sand called a *tanour*. A wood fire is lit in the *tanour*. When the fire turns to ashes, the meat is wrapped in leaves and put in and is covered over with sand. After 24 hours, the meat is beautifully tender. It is served on a large dish surrounded by rice and dates. The dish is placed on the ground and everyone sits around it in a circle. The food is always eaten with the right hand. Traditionally, the host offers his guest the choicest pieces.

An Arab meal always ends with coffee, and the traditional preparation of coffee is a symbol of Arab hospitality. The beans are roasted over a fire before being ground with a pestle and mortar. Water is added to the ground coffee and it is brought to a boil. Sometimes a few cardamom seeds are added, and the coffee is boiled again. It is poured from a *dallah,* a long-spouted coffee pot which is usually made of brass or copper. The coffee is served in small cups without handles. Only a little coffee is poured into each cup. As soon as the guest has finished it, the cup is handed back to the host to be refilled. It is good manners to drink more than one cup. The host will go on refilling the cup until the guest "jiggles" it to show that he has had enough. Since alcohol is forbidden by Islam, coffee is a favorite social drink. Coffee is served on all occasions: in the ruler's *majlis* (audience room), in the home, in the office, and often even in shops.

A wedding in the UAE usually lasts about three days. It is customary to marry a relative. The bride is usually in her late teens.

A wedding in Ras al Khaimah. Weddings in the UAE usually last about three days and celebrations are on a large scale.

Although her marriage will be arranged by her parents, she may refuse to marry a man who is not acceptable to her.

Wedding celebrations are always on a large scale, with plenty of traditional music and dancing. At celebrations, musicians play drums, *taarah*, and *jerba* to accompany the singers. The *taarah* is a tambourine made of goatskin; the *jerba* is a bagpipe made from an

43

Arab musicians playing traditional instruments.

inflated goatskin. Sometimes young girls dance between two rows of singers, swinging their long, silky black hair.

At the time of her marriage, a girl is given a dowry by her husband. The dowry is usually a considerable sum of money. The bride keeps this even if she is divorced or widowed. A woman's rights are strictly safeguarded. If she is divorced, she returns to her father's household.

Often in the past the bridegroom gave his bride a large wooden chest in which to keep her clothes and jewelry. These chests used to be a typical piece of furniture in Arab homes. They were very heavy, being made of teak or mahogany. Brass plated and studded varieties are known as Kuwaiti chests. Sometimes the brasswork was highly decorative and elaborate. The chests often had a secret compartment under a false bottom.

Arab jewelry is now usually made of gold, but the traditional jewelry of the Bedouin was made of silver which probably came from Iran. It was heavy and intricately worked, and often had a practical use. The men wore belts of woven silver thread. The decorated *khanjar*, or curved dagger, hung from the belt. The women carried *kohl* (a cosmetic used like today's eyeshadow) in little silver pots. Silver charm cases, with verses from the Koran sealed inside them, hung on chains around the neck. Heavy anklets and bracelets were worn, and a specific ring for each finger. Tiny objects were often put into hollow silver jewelry to rattle rhythmically with a dancer's movements.

Henna is also associated with weddings and with Eid festivities. It is grown on a bush. The henna berry is dried and ground, and forms a rich red paste when mixed with water. It is used as a form of make-up. On the eve of her wedding, intricate patterns are painted on the hands and feet of the bride. It is also believed that henna possesses medicinal properties and it is sometimes rubbed into the hair to cure headaches.

Folklore has it that Fatima, the daughter of the Prophet Muhammad, was once invited to the wedding of some wealthy people. At the wedding she was mocked for her poverty but the Prophet sent the angels to his daughter with a beautiful dress, a gift of money for the bride, and henna for her own decoration.

The loose-fitting clothes worn by the men and women of the UAE are well adapted to the hot climate. The various layers provide insulation against the heat, and their movement gives a cool-

A bride's hands, painted with intricate patterns in henna.

ing effect. Most of the local men wear a long white gown, called a *dishdasha*, and a head cloth called a *ghutra*. In summer, the ghutra is normally a thin white cloth, while in winter thicker colored ones called *shemaghs* are used. A skullcap is usually worn under the ghutra. A twisted black coil (*agul*) holds the ghutra in place. Sometimes a flowing white or brown cloak known as a *bisht* is worn. It is usually made from camel's wool, and it is edged with gold braid.

Women in the UAE wear loose baggy trousers called *sirwal* under long dresses called *kandura*. The dresses are often embroidered around the neck, sleeves, and hem with gold or silver

46

thread. Over the kandura is the *thaub,* a rectangular piece of cloth with holes for the arms and head. When women go out, they wear a black cloak (*abaya*) which covers them from head to foot. The Islamic religion requires women to cover their hair in public. Most women also wear veils, and some wear masks called *burqas.*

The women are not only kept apart from men by their clothing. Every house or tent provides a segregated area called a harem. Arab houses are traditionally built around a central courtyard. Often there is a set of two doors to provide a lobby to ensure that guests cannot see directly into the courtyard. The women of the house often go in and out by another door at the back of the house. A male guest would be shown into the *majlis*—a room for receiving guests. A bathroom would adjoin the majlis so that the guest could be entertained without disturbing the privacy of the

A woman in Ras al Khaimah wearing the *abaya*—a long black cloak which covers her from head to foot.

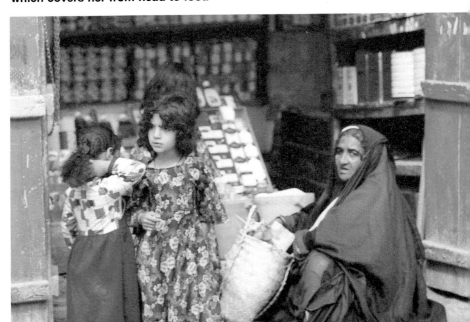

rest of the house. Traditionally, only a father, a brother, a son, and possibly other very close male relatives, may go beyond the majlis to speak with the women of the household.

The family meets in the courtyard, the central area of the house. All the rooms open onto it. There is often a well in the courtyard and cooking is done there. The roof of the house is flat, and it is screened and walled on the outside to provide more space. It is sometimes used for sleeping in summertime. Walls are high, and there are no windows onto the street, or only very small ones high up.

Oil revenue has brought water and electricity to even the most remote areas of the UAE. Nevertheless, the village women still go about their daily routine much as they have always done, although today many of them have Pakistani or Baluchi servants to help them. The women spend their time cooking and tending to the animals. A woman never milks a camel; this is traditionally a man's job. In the afternoons the women spin and weave. In the past they made rugs and tents. Nowadays they usually make camel trappings to decorate the camels for the races, for every village has its race track.

Before the introduction of modern low-cost housing, the majority of people on the coast lived in palm-frond houses which were cooled by the sea breeze. In inland towns and villages, houses were made of mud bricks. The people from the coast of what is now Iran introduced the *badgeer* or windtower. This was perhaps the earliest form of air conditioning. The Bastakia area of Dubai still contains many of these decorative and distinctive towers. It is

A *badgeer*, or windtower—an early form of air-conditioning introduced to the UAE from Persia (the country we now know as Iran).

called Bastakia because the builders were merchants from Bastak in southern Iran. The tower is divided diagonally to form four triangular shafts. When wind, from any direction, hits one of the walls it is tunneled down the hollow shaft to the room below, where increased air movement makes the people more comfortable.

6

Animals of the UAE

There are five different habitats in the UAE: the mountains, the *wadis*, the gravel plains (which run along the foothills of the mountains), the sand desert, and the coastal belt and creeks. Each supports different plants and animals.

The Arabian leopard lives in the isolated Hajar mountains where it eats wild goats and the Arabian tahr, another goatlike animal. Other local carnivores include the wolf and the caracal. All these animals are extremely rare and shy, and few people have seen them.

There used to be many gazelle. The name *Abu Dhabi* means "father of the white gazelle." Herds of oryx once roamed the sands, but in the 1960s, with the introduction of motor vehicles and good guns, the oryx was wiped out in the UAE. However, there are captive populations, and the public can see them in Al Ain zoo. The oryx has a thick white coat, under which is a fatty layer. The skin is black, which cuts down the absorption of ultra-

50

violet rays from the sun. Wide hooves help the oryx to walk in the sand. The animal has two spiral horns, and it has been suggested that tales of unicorns may really have been descriptions of oryx which had lost a horn!

The little fennec fox is still quite common. It burrows underground where it is cooler, while hares find shade beneath a bush or rock. Other small mammals include gerbils, mice, and jerboas. They are nocturnal and burrowers, so also escape the heat. Some spiders, such as the fearsome-looking wolf spider and the camel spider, also come out at night. Scorpions are well-suited to the desert conditions. Their hard outer skeletons conserve moisture. In their tails they have a poisonous sting which kills their prey; then they absorb the body juices of their victims. With their jagged claws, they too burrow to keep cool.

More than 50 varieties of reptiles have been recorded in the UAE. They live happily in desert areas because they are cold-blooded, and they are able to take on the temperature of their surroundings. Their scaly skins retain moisture, and they find most of the water they need in the food that they eat. There are many toads in the wadis, and in the breeding season thousands of tadpoles can be seen in the streams. Of the snakes, only a few are poisonous and bites are rare.

The carnivorous monitor lizard lives in the open desert and grows up to four feet (1.2 meters) long. The thorny-tailed agama lizard inhabits the gravel plains. Although only half the size of the monitor, it looks fierce with sharp teeth, strong jaws, a long spiky

The thorny-tailed agama lizard which inhabits the gravel plains.

tail which it lashes vigorously, and an ability to inflate its body and hiss loudly. However, it is in fact a vegetarian! The most common reptile is probably the gecko. Most houses play host to a few of these sandy-colored lizards, and they are usually welcomed since they eat the insects.

Some freshwater fish live in the mountain wadis, and the sea is rich in marine life. The dugong (a seal-like sea-cow) is seen, but only rarely. It was this creature which inspired tales of mermaids because of the way it floats in the water.

With such a long coastline, the UAE has always been important in the migration of seabirds. A number of birds also live in the oases and date plantations. Today, well over 300 species of birds have been recorded in the UAE. The program of "turning the desert green" has encouraged many more birds to "stop over" and some of them also breed in the UAE. Planting has produced vegetable matter which attracts insects, and they in turn attract the birds. The UAE is in an excellent position for birds migrating from Europe to Africa and from Asia to Africa to stop and take a rest. Many have found the Emirates a good place in which to winter. Few birds spend the entire year here, but some of those which are frequently seen are palm doves, house sparrows, parakeets, mynahs, and hoopoes. The Egyptian vulture lives and breeds in the mountains near Al Ain. There are also four varieties of big, impressive-looking eagles.

Since bees are native to the desert, the bee-eater can also be found here. It is an interesting bird. It wipes the bee on the branch of a tree in order to knock off the insect's sting. Since it is not immune to bee stings, it plays safe and treats all insects in this way. The "butcher" bird is also seen here. It impales its food on the spikes of thorn trees.

Along the coast, millions of Socotra cormorants and black-headed gulls can be seen. Waders, such as herons and flamingos, are also found in abundance. Dubai's creek attracts the flamingos, and a man-made island is being planned for them.

His Highness Sheikh Mohammed bin Rashid al Maktoum established the Dubai Wildlife Research Center in 1982. The center specializes in projects aimed at conserving the wildlife of the Arabian region. A remarkable record of rearing hubara bus-

53

tards from wild-laid eggs has been achieved. In this way, stocks of hubara depleted by hunting can be replenished.

The bird most often associated with Arab countries is, perhaps, the falcon. For centuries, falconry has been the most popular way of hunting small game. Falconry probably originated in the steppes and dunes of Central Asia. It grew in importance in the Islamic world following the Muslim conquests, which brought the Arabs into contact with Byzantines and Persians.

The peregrine falcon, renowned for its courage and high flight, is a favorite. It is caught in the Emirates on its autumnal migration from Pakistan to Africa. Sakers and lanners are also used.

The chief quarry in the Emirates is the hubara or MacQueen's bustard. The hubara is several times larger than the hawk, and the sport is rarely one-sided. It can squirt a slime onto the hawk's feathers and eyes. The hawk is temporarily blinded, and the sticky substance glues its feathers together so that it cannot fly properly. Sometimes the hubara will sit perfectly still, hoping that the hawk will not spot him, but a well-trained hawk knows its quarry is lying low, and bides its time. Even when cornered, the hubara will put up a hard fight. Sometimes it manages to outfly the hawk, and the falconer must call back his bird by swinging the lure. A good hawk can take up to nine hubara in a day.

There are two traditional methods of catching falcons. One is to erect a thin net and loosely peg it to the ground in an area where the birds are known to hunt. A pigeon is tied under the net to

Falconry is still the most popular way of hunting small game in the UAE.

attract the falcon. When the falcon dives down on its prey, the net is pulled from the ground and the bird becomes entangled in it.

In the second method a captive pigeon is again used to attract the falcon. This time the Bedouin digs a pit and hides in it, holding a string attached to the decoy pigeon. When the falcon is sighted, the pigeon is encouraged to flutter. The falcon swoops on the pigeon and kills it. Sometimes a net is employed. The Bedouin jerks another string and the net snaps over the bird. Otherwise, the Bedouin simply eases the dead pigeon, with the falcon feeding on it, toward the pit. When the falcon is sufficiently close, it is caught by the legs. A great deal of time and patience is required to trap a bird. Female birds are preferred because they are larger, as is the case with all birds of prey.

A bird can be trained in two to three weeks. Her eyelids are sealed with thread and she is hooded with a leather cap or *burqa*. This cuts off the sight of any alarming movements. The eyelids are gradually unsealed as she becomes familiar with her owner. Stepping onto the fist is encouraged by tempting her with meat. As the bird becomes tamer, her owner calls her along a line tied to the *jesses* on her legs. The jesses are straps, usually made of leather. However, the Bedouin of the Emirates braid the straps from camel or goat's hair since the humidity in the climate

"Manning" a falcon. This is part of a falcon's training, enabling it to get used to people and noise.

encourages mold growth on leather. The falcon is trained to come to a lure made of hubara wings which it quickly learns to associate with the meals it gets when it lands on the lure.

Under Islamic law a Muslim cannot eat "dead" meat, that is, meat that has not been killed specifically for the purpose of eating. However, the Koran allows the falcon's kill to be eaten if the hunter releases his bird "in the name of Allah." The falcon is allowed a bite at her kill, but then the kill is cunningly removed. If the falcon were allowed to satisfy her appetite, she would not hunt again that day.

Falcons can reach 20 years old. Some hunt right up until they are 18. At the end of winter, 80 percent of the birds are traditionally released back into the wild. Only the star performers are kept. Although some birds fetch very high prices, to an Arab their worth is immeasurable.

Dubai now boasts a falcon hospital, the first of its kind in the world, built by Finance and Industry Minister H. H. Sheikh Hamdan bin Rashid al Maktoum. It was initially run by an American veterinary surgeon who was a keen falconer himself. The hospital is equipped with a special X-ray unit. In the laboratory, blood samples are examined. Culture and sensitivity tests are carried out to make sure that the bacteria are sensitive to a medicine, so that the right antibiotic is prescribed for each sick bird. Some innovative surgery is also performed at the hospital. A common ailment is infected feet (known to the Bedouin as *somal* or "bumble foot"), when the feet have been accidentally pierced by

Treating a falcon at the Dubai Falcon Hospital, the first of its kind in the world.

the bird's talons. After surgery, the bird is fitted with a hollowed-out plaster cast and looks as if she is wearing a high-heel shoe. This clever device ensures that there is no pressure on the foot. Falcons sometimes suffer from fungus of the lungs. This is treated in an oxygen cage, as we would treat a patient with pneumonia in an oxygen tent.

At the height of the hunting season, in December, there may be as many as 35 birds in the hospital. People bring their birds to the hospital from all over the Gulf region.

The birds are fed once a day on quails, since quails quickly convert food into body weight. Once a week, sometimes more, the falcons are encouraged to kill the quails for themselves. Otherwise, being very sensitive birds, falcons can become unhappy and self-destructive. Just as nervous people will bite their nails, so a falcon will bite its claws. They are flown every day, and their quarters are "carpeted" with sand to make them feel at home. The peregrines at the hospital live in modified daylight, and they are given extra hormones to encourage them to molt since the climate in the UAE is poor for molting.

Deserts are the most difficult places in the world for animals to survive. The days are long and hot, there is little water and often food is scarce. So creatures which live here have developed ways of coping with these problems. One animal which is ideally suited to its surroundings is the camel. No one knows when camels were first domesticated but today there are none in the wild, nor have there been for hundreds of years. Every camel in the UAE is accounted for and has its owner's mark upon it to prove it.

The camel used by the Bedouin of the UAE is the dromedary or one-humped camel. It well deserves its nickname of "ship of the desert." Its large flat feet can move easily over the sand without sinking. It will always sit facing the sun so that the smallest amount of body area is exposed to the sun's rays. During the heat of the day, it conserves its energy by sitting quite still, with much of its body resting in the cooler ground below the top soil. Its hump stores fat, which can be used to supply energy if needed. The camel's hump is a sign of its physical condition. When the camel is well-fed, its hump is plump and firm. The hump sags as the fat is used up when food is scarce. A camel can drink as much as 27 gallons (120 liters) of water at a time. In other animals, the blood cells would burst and the animal would die. But a camel loses water from its tissues and not from its blood so there is no strain on its heart. If it lacks water, it can adjust its body temperature to that of its surroundings, and thereby avoid sweating. It can go for several days without food and water, and even in the height of summer has been known to survive for as long as 17 days without water.

In the desert, water is usually found some distance below the surface and has to be drawn up in goatskin bags. Imagine how many bags of water each camel drinks. Watering a herd of perhaps 50 camels in summertime would be very hard work indeed. But in the winter camels may go for six, or even seven, weeks without any water if there is enough of the right kind of grazing.

The camel has double rows of long, heavy lashes to protect its eyes from wind-blown sand. It can also close its nostrils to keep out the sand. It has a keen sense of sight and smell. Its coat insulates it against the sun during the day and keeps it warm in the cool of the night.

In the past, the Bedouin's livelihood depended on his camels. For much of the year he lived mainly on camel's milk and dried dates. Camel's milk is high in vitamin C, and a healthy female can give nine pints (five liters) a day as well as suckling her calf.

The camel was also used for riding and as a beast of burden.

The Bedouin traveled light, with rifle and *khanjar* (curved dagger), a few cooking pots, some dried dates, and as many goatskin bags of water as the camels could carry. The Bedouin always thought of his camel's well-being first. The animals would be watered at the wells first. Even when he was in a hurry he would allow his camels to wander for grazing. Nowadays, camels are fed on locally-grown alfalfa, but the boys who look after them still gather the natural desert grasses for them as well. The heat makes salt a necessary ingredient in their diet, and many bushes in the desert are naturally salty.

The camel is, of course, a source of meat; its wool is used for making rugs, and its hide for making containers. No part of it is wasted—even the dung is used for fuel. Since the female gives milk and is also considered the faster runner, a herd consists mainly of females. The Bedouin generally kill male calves for a festive occasion, such as a wedding. Camels are also traded for rifles, rice, coffee, and jewelry. A Bedouin's camels are a sign of his wealth.

Traditionally, the camel was hobbled by having its front legs tied together to prevent it from wandering too far. The Arabic word for "string" sounds like "hobble," so perhaps this is where the English word comes from. Unfortunately, with more and more cars on the road, the camels sometimes meet their death at the hands of motorists. The wide highway connecting Abu Dhabi Emirate to Dubai Emirate is notorious for this. The long, straight road encourages fast driving but the desert on either side of the road is unlit at nights. A camel will suddenly loom up out of the pitch blackness and shamble into the road. By the time the driver sees it, it is too late.

Another domesticated animal used in the UAE is the donkey. Like the camel, it is a beast of burden, and can be seen even now pulling water carts in remote areas.

Horses are not commonly used in the UAE, as the ground is too soft for their hooves. However, in the past, merchant families in the towns sometimes owned and rode horses. Arab horses are famous throughout the world for their spirit and stamina, and for

A Bedouin watering his camels. In the past, a Bedouin's livelihood depended almost entirely on his camels.

Camels—their long, heavy lashes protect their eyes from sand.

their good looks. They were already known at the time of the Prophet Muhammad. With the spread of Islam, they found their way to North Africa, Spain, and France and, after the Crusades, to Northern Europe, notably Britain. Most sheikhs like to own some, and horses have always been considered a suitable gift between sheikhs.

Sometimes a few cattle are kept in the oases, and in Buraimi oasis oxen are also kept to plow the fields because wheat grows there.

Sheep and goats are still herded in the UAE. Goats are preferred as they eat almost anything. The government pays families an allowance for every animal they raise. The women milk the goats,

A goat for sale at a market. The government pays an allowance for every animal raised and goats are still herded in large numbers.

and some of the milk is turned into curds. The goat hair used to be woven into tent material, and into socks to protect the feet from burning sands. The skins became water carriers. A musical instrument, rather like the Scottish bagpipes, was also fashioned from it. Even the hooves were used. Fastened onto a piece of cloth and worn by the men around their waist and over the hips during traditional dances, they sounded like castanets as they clacked together.

7

From Pearls to Black Gold—Trade and Industry in the UAE

Pearl diving used to be the main occupation of people living along the shores of the Persian Gulf. At the turn of the 19th century, at the pearling trade's peak, a flotilla of some 1,200 boats was home to about 22,000 sailors. This meant that most of the Trucial States's able-bodied male population was engaged in pearling.

Dhow is the general term used to cover all local craft. The pearling boats were called *sambuks*. They were propelled by sails, but they had oars as well. The sambuk was made ready by oiling the upper hull with shark oil, and anti-fouling the lower half of the hull with a mixture of lime and sheep's fat. Supplies of dates, rice, tea, sugar, coffee, and water for the crew were stored on board.

The ship's captain was called the *nakhuda*. He collected together a crew of between 40 and 60 men and set out for the diving place, known as the *heer*. The life of the diver was hard and dangerous. Hazards of the sea included giant stingrays, swordfish, and jellyfish. To prevent himself from being stung the diver sometimes wore a white cotton suit. Leather finger stalls, called *khabt,* protected his fingers. A leather socket covered the big toe of his right foot which the diver used to push his way along the seabed. He pinched his nose with a peg of horn or bone to keep out the water. His only other equipment was a knife to prise the oysters from the seabed, and a basket hung around his neck to carry them in. When he jumped he had two ropes tied around his waist, one weighted to sink him, the other by which his assistant, the *saib,* could pull him up.

Work began shortly after sunrise. First, the oysters caught the previous day would be opened. Perhaps one pearl would be found in 4,000 oysters. A dive might last a minute and a half, though an experienced diver could stay under water for up to four minutes. The more perfect pearls generally came from the deeper water. After a few minutes' rest, the diver would go down again. This routine could continue for six to eight hours. Diving was not permitted during Ramadan.

Pearls were sold to the *tawwash,* the buying merchant, accompanied by traditional bargaining. The captain negotiated the sale, but he was accompanied by two of his crew to see fair play. Negotiations were carried out through finger language under a piece of cloth in order to keep the deal private. The merchant used delicate scales and weights of the semiprecious stones agate and cornelian. The pearls were sieved for size through small perforated copper basins.

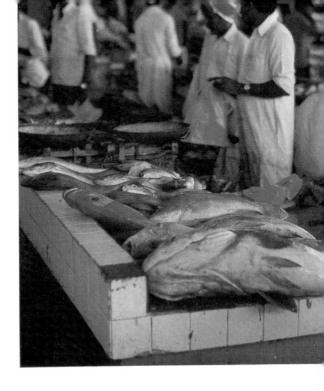

A fish market. Fish is still the staple diet of many Arabs in the UAE.

During the last century, Gulf merchants sent their pearls to Bombay which was the great eastern center of the trade. Buyers from Europe and New York called there regularly.

By 1940 the pearl trade had almost disappeared due to Japan's development of the cultured pearl and the lack of demand for such luxuries as pearls during the Depression of the 1930s. However, fishing has continued to be an important source of livelihood, especially in the northern emirates.

The variety of fish found in and around the coast is enormous. Fishermen can be at sea for as long as a week before returning to the fish markets with their catches. The annual catch is about 70,000 tons, some of which is dried and exported.

Fish has always been a favorite food of the Gulf Arabs. In the past, it was the main source of protein for many people. However, some popular varieties of fish have decreased in supply. For this reason, the UAE government, with Japanese assistance, set up the country's first fish-farming project. The National Mariculture Center is in Umm al Qawain. There are 40 ponds of different sizes for breeding popular varieties. The center also comprises a laboratory and an aquarium, where about 50 species of Gulf fish are on display.

The transformation of the UAE's economy began in 1962 with the first export of oil from Abu Dhabi.

This "black gold" was formed under the surface of the earth millions of years ago. It has long been known to man, yet it is only during the past hundred years or so that we have realized its usefulness.

Today, oil is used for transportation and heating, and in the manufacture of fertilizers, fabrics, medicines, plastics, pesticides, paints, and thousands of other items. No wonder, then, that having such a precious commodity makes a country powerful.

The Middle East is one of the main oil-producing regions in the world, extracting about one-third of the world's oil. The UAE, however, was a latecomer to the ranks of the world's major oil-exporting countries with Abu Dhabi exporting its first barrel of oil only in 1962. The government of the Abu Dhabi emirate has a monopoly over distribution and is responsible for all petroleum installations and oil-based industries in the emirate.

Dubai is the second largest producer in the UAE. The emirate of Dubai also owns controlling interest in the oil production in its territory. When oil was found in Dubai, Fateh was the first oil field. Sheikh Rashid personally named the field when it was discovered in 1966. *Fateh* means "good fortune" in Arabic.

The Mubarak offshore oil field in Sharjah was discovered in 1972 but the first shipment was not exported until almost two years later. The field's production capacity gradually fell. However, in December 1980, a much-needed boost came with Amoco's discovery of a major oil and gas field just a short distance from Sharjah itself.

In the emirate of Ras al Khaimah, oil was struck in the Saleh field, some 26 miles (42 kilometers) offshore, in February 1983. The other emirates continue to grant concessions for oil and gas exploration.

In the 1990s, Abu Dhabi produced about 1,750,000 barrels a day—that is 70 percent of the UAE's output. A large proportion of crude oil is exported, mainly to Japan. The United States, France, and the Netherlands are also major customers, and Britain and Germany take a small amount.

At present, Abu Dhabi and Dubai are the main producers of liquefied natural gas in the Gulf. The gas is separated into liquid gas—propane and butane—and dry gas. Liquid gas is exported mainly to Japan, where it is used in the manufacture of chemicals and fuels. The residue dry gas is used to supply local industry.

The UAE has numerous desalination plants. Desalination is the process by which fresh water is obtained from seawater. This is done by heating the seawater so that some of it evaporates, forming water vapor. The vapor rises and is piped into colder con-

An offshore oil-rig. The discovery of this "black gold" has transformed the economy of the UAE.

denser tubes. It drops as distilled water into trays, and is then led away for blending to produce drinking water. For every unit of fresh water produced eight units of seawater are used. Desalination is very important in the desert, where water supply from rainfall is insufficient.

At Jebel Ali there are also cement works, a structural steelwork fabrication workshop, a 300-megawatt steam power station, and an electrical cable plant. It was envisaged that this extensive industrial development, 22 miles (35 kilometers) southwest of Dubai, would serve as the oil field supply and distribution center for the Middle East. The central facility is the largest manmade port in the world.

Mina Jebel Ali can take 67 ships and has nine miles (15 kilometers) of quays. It was completed toward the end of 1980. The port has been designated a Free Trade Zone to encourage trading and re-exporting in the Middle East. Some of the benefits include exemption from taxes, duty-free import of machinery and materials needed for industry, and no currency restrictions. Cargo can be placed in storage, duty-free, until favorable market conditions arise. In the Free Trade Zone there is a modern container terminal, extensive transit storage areas and warehouses. There is also a temperature-controlled warehouse for delicate cargoes which would deteriorate in ordinary storage conditions.

Before the oil boom, the coastline of the UAE had few harbors and ports. The shallow waters and sandy flats meant that large oceangoing tankers had to lie offshore and transfer their cargo into lighter vessels. Prior to harbor developments in Abu Dhabi, Dubai was the only port of entry for merchandise. For centuries, there was a thriving pearling and trading port in Dubai, sheltered in the natural creek. The ancient *dhows* still ply the creek today. The UAE depends heavily on imports for its development needs. Imports through Dubai increased sevenfold between 1964 and 1972. Today, two-thirds of the UAE's imports pass through Dubai. Japan is the leading supplier. The United States, the European Union, Australia, and Singapore are also major suppliers.

One of the first things the emir of Dubai decided to do with oil revenue was to build a 15-berth port. Even before its completion,

An aerial view of the Abu Dhabi gas liquefaction plant.

however, it became clear that it would need to be larger to meet the needs of Dubai's expanding trade. The number of berths was increased to 37. Completed in October 1972, it was appropriately named Port Rashid.

Sharjah and Ras al Khaimah also have ports, while Khor Fakkan, an enclave of Sharjah emirate on the east coast, has a deep-water container terminal. At Jebel Dhanna, in Abu Dhabi emirate, there is the vital oil export terminal.

Dubai's strategic location near the entrance of the Persian Gulf makes it the ideal site for a ship repair yard for the many ships using the oil route. In December 1973, work began on the dry dock. One of the largest in the world, it stands at the mouth of Dubai Creek. Today, tugs help to bring ships into the port, where they can be cleaned and repaired. The dry dock is equipped to

72

repair even the largest tanker afloat. It is particularly suitable for heavy offshore equipment, such as the jack-up platforms, derricks, and pipe-laying barges so vital to the oil fields. At the other end of the creek lies another docking yard which opened in July 1978. Here traditional Arab *dhows* are repaired alongside huge cargo liners.

A symbol of the UAE's trading history is the World Trade Center Tower in Dubai. This 39-story, 650-foot (200-meter) high tower is a striking landmark which dominates the skyline. It opened in 1979 and houses over numerous national and international companies. The complex also includes some consulates, a hotel, apartment blocks, and exhibition halls. Businessmen come here from Saudi Arabia, Kuwait, Bahrain, Qatar, Oman, and even further afield.

A vital feature of trade is banking. The unit of currency in the UAE is the *dirham*. This was created in 1973 to replace the Bahraini dinar and the Qatar/Dubai *riyal* which had been used previously in the Emirates.

Foreign banks flocked to the UAE in the 1970s and banking grew out of proportion to the population. In 1973 a central monetary authority, the UAE Currency Board, was established. This was replaced in 1980 by the Central Bank. The rulers of Abu Dhabi and Dubai agreed to place half of their national revenues with the new institution. This example of unity gives the Central Bank the federal support which the Currency Board lacked. The Central Bank has the power to regulate operations of the financial system. Banking can no longer grow in the previous uncontrolled

An aerial view of Port Rashid.

way. Restrictions have been enforced so that all foreign banks have had to reduce the number of their branches to a maximum of eight. Now banking is dominated by national banks. In 1983, the Emirates Industrial Bank was established to provide loans to new and expanding industries. In 1991 the international Bank of Credit and Commerce had to be closed due to internal corruption.

Though the economy of the UAE depends heavily on oil and oil-based industries, the government is well aware of the dangers of relying on one single source of income. One of the aims of the Chambers of Commerce is to encourage new industries. Industrial development has come in a natural manner in tune with emerging needs. Consequently, a number of plants were established to manufacture building materials in order to meet the

74

needs of the construction boom. Cement factories sprang up through the Emirates. The largest is in Ras al Khaimah. Using the rocks of the Hajar mountains, Ras al Khaimah has also established an export business in aggregates (the broken stones and other materials used in making concrete). Light industries in the UAE include the manufacture of ballpoint pens, paper bags, rope, paint, and foam.

Similarly, many plants were established for manufacturing foodstuffs in order to supply the market with local products in place

Dubai dry dock.

of imported ones. These include ice cream, cooking oil, nuts, crisps, and canned drinks. Dairies produce milk, yogurt, labneh (a thick, creamy curd), and cheese. There are plants which bottle mineral waters from the freshwater springs at Ras al Khaimah, Masafi, and Hatta. At the same time, great attention has been paid to agriculture.

The World Trade Center Tower in Dubai.

8

Turning the Desert Green

Traditionally, agriculture in the UAE centered on the nomads, who traveled the deserts in search of pasture for their animals, and on small oases, where crops such as dates could be grown.

Dates are still a major crop. The date palm has separate male and female plants and is propagated from root suckers produced by the female plants. The fruit is high in caloric value and used to be the staple food for men and beasts on long journeys through the desert. The tree trunks were used in the construction of houses, and branches were bound together to make a lightweight building material known as *barasti*. The leaves were woven to make baskets.

Date gardens were planted where watering by *aflaj* was possible. *Aflaj* are ancient underground water channels which were probably constructed in pre-Islamic times. The *falaj* (the singular of *aflaj*) brings water from its source to the date gardens where it comes to the surface. The flow can then be directed and regulated.

A *falaj* or irrigation channel.

In *falaj*-irrigated gardens, a few other fruit trees grew among the date palms. Oranges, lemons, and limes were the most common. Mangoes, figs, mulberries, bananas, and pomegranates also seemed to do well and grapes were sometimes grown over trellises. Beneath the trees, several crops of alfalfa (a crop grown to feed cattle and camels) could be harvested each year, and some vegetables also grew.

Date gardens in desert locations grew without *falaj* irrigation, for the roots of the date palms quickly reached down to the water table. However, the resulting fruits were smaller. *Barasti* fencing protected the gardens from drifting sand.

78

In Ras al Khaimah and Fujeirah, better rainfall and a higher underground water table made a larger amount of land cultivable. Here, the traditions of fishing and date farming were largely untouched by the oil boom.

Despite the extreme aridity of most of the UAE, the country is now producing a large proportion of its own food. Experiments both in cattle raising and in growing a variety of crops prove steadily more successful. Farmers and agriculturalists have come up with ingenious irrigation systems, greenhouses that keep the heat out rather than in, and hydroponic farms. This last is a system whereby plants are grown without soil in plastic tubes. They are kept in temperature-controlled greenhouses and fed by liquids pumped through the tubes. Tomatoes and cucumbers grown in this way can be harvested after a few weeks.

Digdagga Agricultural Trial Station was set up in 1955 in Ras al Khaimah to find out which crops would grow best in the harsh climate. Various vegetables and fruit trees were tried out. An agricultural school was opened. Today cabbages, onions, tomatoes, dates, bananas, and citrus fruits are grown in the area.

Another flourishing agricultural center is Al Ain oasis. Here about 1,200 acres of land has been made cultivable. Many of them were developed at the government's expense and then allocated to the people. Agricultural guidance centers and veterinary centers encourage the country's farmers, and the government helps with the cost of fertilizers, seeds, and pesticides.

In 1975 the government asked the United Nations Food and Agricultural Organization (FAO) to help. Their findings assisted

Date palms in Fujeirah.

the UAE in planning for the future. FAO experts trained local people to continue the work.

Experiments to discover the most suitable methods of irrigation are particularly important in the desert where water is scarce. It has been found that drip irrigation works best for rows of vegetable crops; the bubbler system for fruit trees; and sprinklers for alfalfa, onions and potatoes. Rhodes grass, from Kenya, is also grown and made into hay. Imagine climbing to the top of a desert sand dune and finding a field of wheat stretched out below you. That is what you would find at Al Oha near Al Ain. Such a surprise is no longer as uncommon as it might sound in the UAE.

The number of farmers in the UAE increased from over 7,500 in 1977 to 5 percent of the workforce in 1996. Production of field crops, fruit production, and vegetable production rose considerably. Vegetables grown in the UAE include cabbages, beans, lettuce, eggplant (aubergines), tomatoes, peppers, cucumbers, and potatoes. Tobacco is also grown. Ras al Khaimah and Fujeirah produce a variety of fruits ranging from lemons to bananas and mangoes. Watermelon and sweet melon also thrive.

There are a number of poultry and dairy farms in the UAE. Supermarkets now stock locally produced eggs and chickens, and the country is well on its way to self-sufficiency in this area. Fresh milk and yogurt come from Al Ain, Umm al Qawain, and Al Marmum in the emirate of Dubai, as well as from Digdagga. Dairies use an instant cooling system to make fresh milk last longer.

The rapid expansion of agriculture meant that many new wells

Market stalls full of locally grown produce—the result of a dramatic increase in agricultural production.

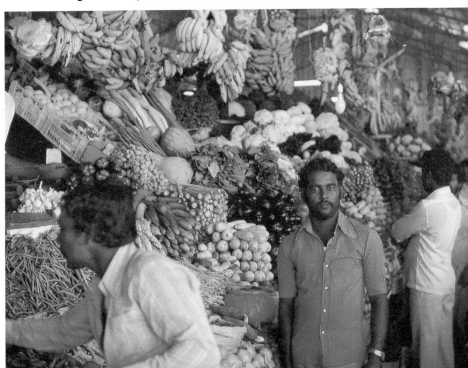

were dug for irrigation. This resulted in the level of the water table dropping dramatically in many areas. To cope with this, the production of desalinated water has been increased. The government now controls the drilling of wells. Another major step is the construction of dams to catch the water from the mountains which would otherwise rush down the wadis to the sea. Progress is also being achieved in the recycling of sewage to provide water to irrigate parks and gardens. Sheikh Zayid dreamed of turning the desert green, and this no longer seems as unlikely as it sounds. So far, Abu Dhabi, the nation's capital, is the greenest city, but this greenness is fast spreading throughout the UAE.

"Sweet soil" (that is fertile desert soil untainted by salt from the sea) is brought to sites; then organic matter—such as treated sludge or cow dung—is added to it to nourish it. The municipali-

Sheikh Zayed's dream of "turning the desert green" has led to colorful parks and gardens being planted throughout the Emirates.

ties run nurseries to provide shrubs, plants, and trees for public parks and gardens. City residents can obtain plants free or at minimal cost for their own gardens. Roadsides in the Emirates are now ablaze with color, as periwinkles, sun-plants, and marigolds bloom. Bougainvillea is probably the most colorful garden plant, while oleander, jasmine, and hibiscus also thrive. Leafy Indian almond trees and tall eucalyptus flourish and give shade. All this in a land which not so long ago was little more than sand.

9

The Facilities and Achievements of the UAE

There is no use for money if it is not dedicated to the service of the people.

PRESIDENT SHEIKH ZAYID

With the discovery of oil, and the ensuing wealth, the UAE has developed at an amazing pace. The federal government has constructed a welfare system to match any in the world.

The country's first school opened in Sharjah in 1953. In 1971, education was made compulsory, for boys and girls alike, from the age of six. Education is free for all nationals, even for those studying abroad. Meals, uniforms, and textbooks are also free. Each child receives pocket money which increases with his progress at school each year. In addition, parents receive a monthly allowance for each child who is attending full-time school.

The government's policy is to take the benefits of modern civilization out to the Bedouin, rather than force the Bedouin to come to the cities. There are now a number of small schools in

A girls' school in Abu Dhabi. Education is free for all children in the UAE.

remote rural areas. And, in this way, the Bedouin's traditional way of life is not disrupted.

Besides government-owned schools there are a number of private schools in the UAE. English-speaking education is also available, and there are schools of other nationalities including French, German, and Japanese. In accordance with Islam, coeducation among Muslims is only at the very youngest ages, and instruction in the Islamic religion is compulsory. Evening classes for adults are also encouraged.

In 1977, the country's first university opened in Al Ain, United

Arab Emirates University. It started with four faculties: Humanities and Social Sciences, Natural Sciences, Education and Public Administration, and Political Science. The faculty of Islamic Law was added in 1978, and those of Agriculture and Engineering during 1980-1981. Today women make up more than half the student body. The majority of students are from the UAE itself; others come from other parts of the Gulf region.

Many students also go abroad every year to study in other Arab countries, or in Europe or America. In addition, there are training facilities in many of the large companies, especially in the oil sector. In this way the UAE is able to rely more and more on its own trained people to fill important posts.

The government is also making efforts to train women as educators and teachers, and thus reduce dependence on foreign teaching staff. The Ministry of Labor and Social Affairs supports and promotes the progress of local women. Her Highness Sheikha Fatima, the president's wife, heads the UAE Women's Federation. Eleven Social Development Centers in the Emirates provide teaching in health, nutrition, child care, language-training in Arabic and English, cultural and religious lectures, and demonstrations. Local traditional handicrafts are encouraged. They include weaving, talli work (a type of braiding used to decorate local costume), and plaiting date palm fibers which are sewn together to form mats, bowls, and baskets.

Other women are employed by the police force. They handle criminal investigations concerning women and juveniles. They also conduct airport searches of women and driving tests for

Weaving and *talli* work—examples of traditional handicrafts which are being encouraged by the government of the UAE.

women. Some women are also involved in broadcasting in the UAE.

Every community of more than 1,000 people in the UAE has its own clinic; and special traveling clinics visit the nomadic Bedouin in the desert. Each emirate has at least one hospital. Some of the most modern and well-equipped hospitals in the world are to be found in Abu Dhabi, Dubai, and Al Ain.

At the time of independence, the UAE was prone to a number

Policewomen on parade in Dubai.

of fatal diseases. Now, with a thorough preventive medicine program, cholera, typhoid, and tuberculosis are gradually being elim-
inated. The UAE was one of the first countries in the Middle East
to be declared free of smallpox. The country can also boast its
own medical pioneer, Dr. Moinul Haq, who invented the tech-
nique of grafting fish corneas into human eyes.

Major highways through the desert link the emirates and each
city has a modern road system. The UAE is well provided with
port facilities which are vital to a country's prosperity. There are
also three major international airports at Abu Dhabi, Dubai, and

88

Sharjah; and three smaller international airports at Ras al Khaimah, Fujairah, and Al Ain.

Although there is a public bus service in the UAE, taxis are the main form of public transportation. There is no rail system. The majority of families possess at least one car of their own and very often they have a 4-wheel drive vehicle in order to cope with rough terrain in the desert and the rural areas.

There are telephone, cable, and telex facilities throughout the UAE, and the car telephone service is becoming popular. It is possible to dial direct to many different countries all over the world.

There are seven radio stations and eight television stations in the UAE, and Abu Dhabi and Dubai operate English-language services. There is a flourishing Arabic press in the country as well as four English-language daily newspapers.

Dubai airport—one of the three major international airports.

Only a few years ago, power cuts were not uncommon in the Emirates, especially during the hot summer months when air conditioning is in maximum use. Now, power cuts are a thing of the past since power stations have grown to meet the demands. Electricity is subsidized and the government makes sure everyone is provided with good housing, running water, and electricity.

The policy of the country is to share the benefits of its wealth so that the quality of life is improved for everyone–not merely for the nation's own people but for developing countries which require foreign aid. This is a belief based on the precepts of Islam. As a result, the UAE gives generously to countries throughout Africa and Asia.

10

Sports and Leisure

Sports and leisure facilities have been developed to such an extent that the UAE manages to surprise most of its visitors. It is not surprising for the sun and sea to go hand in hand with water sports such as swimming, sailing, windsurfing, waterskiing, fishing, and scuba diving. But Grand Prix car racing, cycling, hockey, and cricket are much more unexpected.

Soccer is definitely the number one sport. Spontaneous games are played on any vacant patch of sand, as well as the organized ones in the splendid stadiums. There is a UAE Soccer Association and the UAE National League is the main feature of the season.

Perhaps the most surprising sport of all to be found in the desert is ice hockey! The first ice rink opened in 1979, and there are regular ice shows, featuring both local and international stars.

Other sports include tennis, polo, squash, netball, basketball, karting, archery, and tenpin bowling. Most of the large hotels house gymnasiums, and there are many well-equipped clubs. An annual raft race takes place every November. The craft are appropriately constructed from empty oil drums! A more traditional race is the long-boat race, with each boat manned by upwards of 80 rowers.

One of the more traditional sports to be found in the UAE is camel racing. A young camel can be trained for racing when it is three to four years old. It is led slowly around the track alongside a more mature camel to set a good example. Camels can be stubborn, and training can take a few months. The rider is always a small, light boy.

At the start of a race, the trainers, mounted on other camels, calm the new racers. There is an unwritten law that a camel may only be whipped into action at the start and the end of a race. A camel averages over 15 miles (25 kilometers) an hour. Nowadays, a trainer sometimes instructs the jockey by closed circuit radio as he watches the race on television from the stand.

Buying a racing camel is carried out with as much care as buying a racehorse. Its feet and legs, its height and girth, are carefully examined. Its lineage, too, is studied. Thoroughbreds have been known to fetch vast sums of money. The most famous pedigree is the Aseel, which means "pure."

Today, camel racing has become a very competitive business, with established racetracks and stadiums. Although betting or gambling is forbidden under Islam, camels may race for prizes. The prizes usually consist of a 4-wheel drive vehicle and a sum of money. Even the smallest village has a camel racing track close by. For sheikh and Bedouin alike, camels and camel racing are a part of the Arab way of life.

A camel race. Camel racing is a major sport in the UAE.

With so much to offer in the way of sporting and leisure facilities, it is not surprising that tourism has begun to play a part in the economy of the UAE. The climate, naturally, has helped to develop this new industry. The sun seekers of Europe can escape from their own cold winters to guaranteed sunshine. This, combined with excellent hotels, beautiful beaches, spectacular scenery, and the country's interesting history and culture, makes for an excellent vacation.

However, the attractions of the UAE are not, as yet, widely known. Sometimes the media reports have an adverse effect on a country. For instance, front-page news of an oil slick in the area is off-putting, even though the beaches of the UAE may not have suffered from it. Again, the Iran-Iraq war was sufficient deterrent to some tourists because of the nearness of Iran to the UAE. The

93

actual border of Iran with Iraq however is some considerable distance from the UAE. However, shipping problems further up the Gulf arising from the war did not make any noticeable impact in the UAE. In fact, problems in Iran's southern ports gave the UAE's facilities a chance to attract new business.

Tourists in the Emirates can go on desert safaris; drive through *wadis*, across mountains and dunes; visit archaeological sites, museums, and forts; see camels and camel races, date gardens, and oases; meet Bedouin in the desert; wander around fascinating *souks*; and pass beautiful mosques, palaces, and picturesque old villages. They can experience for themselves the traditional hospitality of the UAE, exemplified in the age-old greeting: *Ahlan wa-sahlan* ("Hello–Welcome").

Watching a camel race. For sheikh and Bedouin alike, camels and camel racing are a part of the Arab way of life.

GLOSSARY

badgeer	Tower constructed on a house to provide ventilation for cooling
barchans	Crescent shaped sand dunes
dallah	Long-spouted coffee pot made of brass or copper
desalinization	Process which turns seawater into fresh water
dishdasha	Long white gown worn by men
dhows	Great seafaring ships
falaj	System of irrigation channels
forty-day shamal	Seasonal northwest winds that blow over the Gulf area
imam	Muslim spiritual leader
jerba	Bagpipe made from goatskin
Koran	The holy book of the Islamic religion
mosque	Muslim place of worship
nakhuda	Ship captain
oasis	Fertile land in otherwise desert area

polygamy	Having more than one wife or husband
Ramadan	Muslim holy celebration in the ninth lunar month of each year that commemorates the month when the Koran was first revealed to Mohammed
sabkah	Salty mud flats
sheikha	Wife of a sheikh
sirwal	Loose baggy trousers worn by women under their long dresses
sheikhs	Arab chiefs
succulents	Desert plants with fleshy stems to store water
tahr	Goat-like animal that lives in the Hajar Mountains

INDEX

98

Mohammed bin Rashid al
Maktoum, Sheikh, 53
Mosques, 34
Mubarak, 69
Muhammad, Prophet, 19, 32-33, 36,
37, 39, 45
Muslims, 19, 32, 33-39, 57

N
National Mariculture Center, 68
Natural gas, 69

O
OAPEC (Organization of Arab
Petroleum Exporting Countries),
20
Oases, 15
Oil, discovery of, 20, 29, 68-69
Oil production, 69
Oil, revenue from, 20
Oman, 14
OPEC (Organization of Petroleum
Exporting Countries), 20

P
Pearl diving, 65-67
Persian Gulf, 10, 12, 18, 21, 65, 72
Piracy, "Pirate Coast," 28
Plants, 15
Polygamy, 39
Population, 18
Port Rashid, 72
Portuguese, 27, 28

Q
Qatar, 14, 30

Qawasim, 10, 27, 28, 29
Qusais, 24

R
Rainfall, 15
Ramadan, 35-36, 37
Ras al Khaimah, Emirate of, 10, 13,
16, 24, 25, 27, 28, 31, 69, 72, 75,
79, 81, 89
Rashid bin Said al Maktoum,
Sheikh, 30, 69
Religion, 19, 32-39
Reptiles, 51-52
Rub al Khali (Empty Quarter), 14,
15

S
Sabkah, 15
Saudi Arabia, 14
Sharia (Islamic law), 38-39
Sharjah, Emirate of, 13, 16, 28, 69,
72, 84, 88
Shi'ite Muslims, 19
Sports, 91-92
Sunni Muslim, 19
Supreme Council of Rulers of the
Federal Government, 15

T
Tourism, 93-94
Transportation, 88-89
Treaty of Friendship, 31
Trucial Council, 11, 29
Trucial Oman Scouts, 11, 29
Trucial Coast, 29
Trucial States, 11, 12